IMAGES
of America

PATERSON'S
INDUSTRIAL AGE

ON THE COVER: A newly built Rogers locomotive is towed by horses up Market Street past the newly opened city hall and Second National Bank around 1895. (Courtesy of the Paterson Museum, Paterson, New Jersey.)

IMAGES
of America

PATERSON'S
INDUSTRIAL AGE

Richard Polton

ARCADIA
PUBLISHING

Published by Arcadia Publishing
Charleston, South Carolina

Printed in the United States of America

Library of Congress Control Number: 2023943124

For all general information, please contact Arcadia Publishing:
Telephone 843-853-2070
Fax 843-853-0044
E-mail sales@arcadiapublishing.com

Visit us on the Internet at www.arcadiapublishing.com

Immigrants and new arrivals have been essential to the city of Paterson from its founding. This book is dedicated to the generations of immigrants, notably members of my own family, who came to Paterson intent on improving their lives and the future of their children and families. That process continues to this very day.

CONTENTS

Acknowledgments

First, a special thanks and note of appreciation to family and friends who have been supportive and often amused by my love for Paterson. There are Patersonians, past and present, who somewhere in their homes display an image of the Great Falls of the Passaic River as an iconic symbol of their affection for our shared history.

The Paterson Museum and its staff and friends are indispensable in the development of this work. I have relied on the resources of the museum throughout this process. Giacomo DeStefano, the museum director, and Heather Garside are dedicated and knowledgeable leaders who make the most of challenged resources. Glenn Corbett has been a valued advisor. Ed Smyk, Passaic County historian, is dedicated and helpful.

A major impetus for this project has been the formation of the Great Falls National Historical Park, which was taking shape while this book was coming together. The leadership of park superintendent Darren Boch, park ranger Ilyse Goldman, and other colleagues at the National Park Service was essential. The board of the Hamilton Partnership for Paterson (HPP) has been instrumental in bringing the park to fruition. Martin Vergara, board chair, and the executive committee deserve special thanks and appreciation. Leonard Zax, retired president of the HPP, worked for years to make the park a reality. I am particularly grateful to John Lawrence, a friend of long standing who uses his training as a historian for a broad array of good causes. My friends and colleagues at the Jewish Historical Society of Northern New Jersey have been a wonderful resource. Mayor Andre Sayegh, Michael Powell, Gianfranco Archimede, Bob Guarascci, and others in the Paterson administration and community share a passion for Paterson history. Other sources of guidance include Prof. Maxine Laurie of Seton Hall, who was encouraging at key moments.

The local historians of Paterson in the late 19th and early 20th centuries, when Paterson was dynamic and growing, documented the city as they saw it in real time. Notably William Nelson and Charles A. Shriner produced indispensable works about the city's leaders that have been helpful to later generations.

Finally, I am extremely fortunate to have friends and family whom I love and who love me back. Bobbie, our daughters, our sons-in-law, and our grandchildren and cousins are the indispensable part of my life. Introducing the grandkids to the wonders of Paterson and the Great Falls (not to mention fishing the Passaic River with Jake and Henry) is something I cannot stop talking about—perhaps it will be the topic of my next book.

Over the past few years, I have reconnected with my best friends from Paterson Eastside High School. Peter Kornbluth, Bob Fitzgerald, John Lawrence, Peter Levine, and I get on a Zoom call and always find something to talk about. It has been helpful and fun. These were great guys when we got to know each other back then, and they are great friends now. These calls have cemented this friendship.

INTRODUCTION

Paterson is a city that played a major role in the growth of New Jersey and, for that matter, the nation. Although the city was founded by Alexander Hamilton in 1792 as America's first planned industrial city, it took years for the city to truly blossom. The images in this book reflect the years when the city was growing at a record pace.

Paterson's story has held my fascination for years. I grew up here. My family's origins in America are here—two of my grandparents and both of my parents were born here. They all lived the major parts of their life in the city. I grew up in a vibrant community in the Eastside neighborhood. When I went off to college in the mid-1960s, I found a way to incorporate Paterson's history as part of my education, writing about the 1913 Silk Strike for an American history seminar in my senior year. It was an especially timely topic in 1968 at Columbia University.

My interest in Paterson never waned. Years later, I found myself collecting Paterson memorabilia on eBay and at yard sales. A failed effort to purchase a book on Paterson architecture led to a research project on a Paterson architect, Fred Wesley Wentworth, who had a distinguished career that was largely forgotten. A book, dozens of lectures, and multiple walking tours later, I still find the story intriguing and personally significant. During that project, I became familiar with Paterson at the turn of the 20th century.

The city is now the home of the Paterson Great Falls National Historical Park. I have been part of the team planning the visitors center and its exhibits with colleagues from the Hamilton Partnership for Paterson, the National Park Service staff, the Paterson Museum, and the exhibit design firm Ralph Applebaum Associates. It has been gratifying. Our research partner, the Paterson Museum, made available a treasure trove of hundreds of photographic images of the city.

Looking over these memorable photographs, I realized that if properly organized, they told the story of the city in the period from the end of the Civil War to the 1920s. The photographs reflected the high-quality buildings developed during this period in a fast-growing, complicated, vibrant city. I began the process that resulted in this book. The photographs gave substance to the Paterson story of innovation, immigration, changing technologies, disruption, and conflict in an industrializing world. By the mid-19th century, Paterson emerged as one of the most dynamic cities in the nation. It was a hot house of ideas that anticipated much of today's world.

This was a time when belching smokestacks, clogged streets, and the thunderous noise of heavy industry were seen as indicators of progress and precursors to prosperity. By those criteria, Paterson was an absolute wonder. Paterson's various industries were manufacturing powerhouses—it was called a city "with an arm of iron in a sleeve of silk." The factory districts were chockablock with active and vibrant enterprises. People marveled at the noise, the number of people in the workforce, and the quantity and importance of the city's products. The city's population was growing, increasing by 50 percent every decade. The downtown district became a center for commercial businesses, banking, and government. Beautiful commercial buildings, many constructed in the fashionable French Revival style, were shaping the downtown of the "Lyon of America." New residential areas reflecting the growing affluence of the mill owners, merchants, and professionals were transforming open fields into fashionable neighborhoods. The growing population and demand for labor drove housing prices at every price and quality level.

Paterson's business leaders were touting an optimistic story to anyone who would listen. In 1890, the Paterson Board of Trade published a promotional book on Paterson that contained an article called "The Progress of Paterson," a promotional piece designed to attract industry to the city. William G. Fenner, the trade association's vice president with strong ties to the silk industry, explained the city's advantages. For those looking to locate a manufacturing business, Paterson was the perfect place: "It's a location where at least a reasonable certainty of success can be assured their enterprise."

To make his case, Fenner detailed the stories of the successful industries located in the city and offered background on how each type of business had grown. In Fenner's view, Paterson saw constant industrial progress from the early part of the 19th century. First, an active cotton industry (the city's oldest industry) had been operating since the early 1800s. The cotton mills were joined in the 1830s by heavy iron works, machinery fabrication, and locomotive production. Later additions included the nation's largest linen thread plant, followed by more and increasingly innovative machinery shops. Finally, the reigning monarch of Paterson's success was the prosperous silk industry. At that time, Paterson was the source for most of the silk produced in the nation and, for that matter, was one of the largest and most profitable silk producers in the world.

After reviewing the path to Paterson's status as a powerful industrial center, Fenner concluded that once established, the world's great manufacturing cities endure for generations. "Manufacture, like trade, fit themselves to certain locations" and remain profitable. He offered numerous examples: silk has been associated with Lyons in France for generations; Belfast, Ireland, is known for its linen; Manchester, England, is renowned for cotton and wool dress goods; and Sheffield, England, is famous for its cutlery. Other examples are cited of cities identified with industries and products. Once established, he argued, these cities remain dominant and endure for generations. Fenner closed his article by stating:

> In the above, I have shown as a deduction from clearly defined facts that Paterson has steadily increased in her industries and industrial voyage from year to year; furthermore, that her adjacency to New York City, the trade and commercial centre of the country, assumes obvious advantages that are virtually bound to give her an unsurpassed industrial position, the permanence of which is a foregone conclusion, if the uniform experience of countries the world over can be accepted as a guarantee of the future.

The permanence of Paterson's prosperity proved to be relatively short lived. Reality intervened. Within 25 years of the article, the anchor industries described by Fenner that had made Paterson so prosperous in 1880s would largely be a shadow of their former strength. Increasing pressures brought on by automation, needs for efficiency, labor conflicts, lack of land, and miscellaneous other factors would contradict Fenner's assurances of long-lived industrial stability. But in the moment of Fenner's observations, the optimism had strong advocates within the business community. The power of that optimism is reflected in the photographs found in this book.

Architecture is the physical manifestation of contemporary attitudes, hopes, and desires. This confident view of Paterson's future was the mindset for the city that was built in the period from around 1870 to 1920. This was a moment when the people and institutions of Paterson were capable of building a city that would last for generations. They created a place often worthy of their hopes, successes, and ambitions. And they had access to the resources needed to make it happen. Consequently, the core of Paterson's architectural heritage was shaped by this period and built by people who believed that the city would thrive for generations. They were certain the handsome buildings they commissioned would withstand the tests of time.

The photographs of the period reveal a city that produced practical and powerful industrial buildings, developed outstanding commercial and governmental structures, constructed highly designed housing for successful industrialists, and built religious institutions of the highest quality that inspired congregants and nurtured local communities and neighborhoods. Their efforts demonstrate the city's resilience in the face of fire, flood, and economic adversities. This was the Paterson that was built for the present but designed to last for the future.

The business leadership, so optimistic in the 1890s when Fenner was writing his article, found sustaining the city's success difficult. The technological and economic advantages diminished quickly. In short order, waterpower was replaced by newer power sources, and industry could locate anywhere. The silk industry, which seemed so powerful, faced constant pressure to lower production costs, find less expensive places to operate, and adopt new technologies—often at the expense of the city itself. Entrenched conflicts contributed to the industry's ultimate demise. Other major industries had similar highs and lows.

Poverty, slum housing, and other social ills were part of the price Paterson paid. Over the coming decades, Paterson was impacted by a changing economy, housing and highway policies, political infighting, and capital flight. The demographics changed as new groups of residents arrived, worked hard, built communities, and frequently moved on.

And yet, Paterson persists. Changing ethnicities and demographics continue to bring energy to the city's neighborhoods and businesses. The recent efforts at the Paterson Great Falls National Historical Park and Hinchliffe Stadium are examples of the city's potential for progress based on its history and unique character. Paterson is nothing if not authentic and that resonates with many in the region. Several older neighborhoods show examples of revitalization.

Patersonians today continue to deserve a city that inspires and meets their highest aspirations and respects its important history.

One

THE CITY'S HERITAGE

Paterson is a city on the Passaic River, which originates in the wetlands of Morris County. The river meanders through several counties, gathering water from various small tributaries to become a powerful river. Its path travels through a drop in elevation at a break in the Watchung Mountain ridge that forms a mighty falls. The river continues winding its way through the New Jersey landscape before it empties into the Newark Bay. Paterson is the city that grew around the falls, and its story is shaped by the river. Like all of New Jersey, the area was the home of the Lenape people for millennia. Until 1650, the Lenape occupied the forests, rivers, marshes, and paths over a vast area that stretched along the East Coast from western Connecticut to Delaware, including New Jersey and southeastern New York. The first European settlers were the Dutch, who arrived in the area in the late 17th century, forming a small village of farmers and tradesmen. (Courtesy of the Paterson Museum, Paterson, New Jersey.)

HAMILTON

Alexander Hamilton looms large in the Paterson story. As an aide to George Washington during the war, Hamilton and the Continental Army traversed northern New Jersey. In July 1778, Hamilton, along with Washington and others, picnicked on the banks of the falls. The site reportedly left an impression on Hamilton. Once the nation was established, Hamilton rose to a position of authority as the first secretary of the US Treasury Department. Hamilton advocated for an urban industrial development within the American economy. The prospect of a new city dedicated to industry was a Hamilton idea that drew prominent backers, creating what would be called a public-private corporation. The entity was called the Society for Establishing Useful Manufacturers (SUM). Beginning in the 1790s, SUM was granted broad powers to promote an industrial enterprise. Paterson offered several advantages—proximity to New York City and its port, developable land, and, notably, the potential to harness the Great Falls of the Passaic River. And so, it began. (Left, courtesy public domain; below, courtesy of the Paterson Museum, Paterson, New Jersey.)

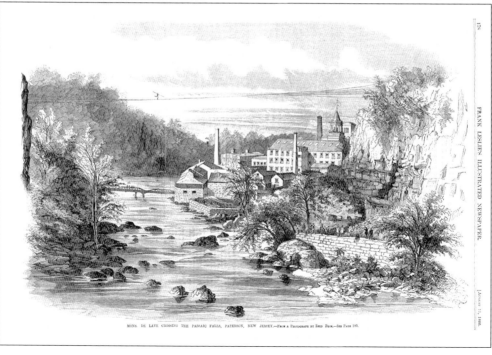

MONS. DE LAVE CROSSING THE PASSAIC FALLS, PATERSON, NEW JERSEY.—FROM A PHOTOGRAPH BY EBID BROS.—SEE PAGE 190.

FRANK LESLIE'S ILLUSTRATED NEWSPAPER.

The SUM board turned to Peter Colt (1746–1824) to lead its operations. Colt arrived in Paterson in 1793, only two years after SUM's founding. Colt had experience as a military aide, merchant, textile manufacturer, and secretary of state of Connecticut. Importantly, he had the confidence of Alexander Hamilton and other leaders of the SUM. They knew that Colt served effectively in the Continental Army, managing the army's supply chain. SUM struggled financially from labor shortages, unanticipated startup costs, and financial misdeeds by board members. Still, work proceeded, and by June 1794, waterpowered manufacturing had begun. Problems persisted and by 1796, the operations went on hiatus despite Colt's competence. For around three years, SUM had limited operations, and its share value shrank. (Courtesy of the Paterson Museum, Paterson, New Jersey.)

74

REID STUDIO

In the early 1800s, Peter Colt recognized that shares in the SUM were undervalued and did not account for its attractive location, waterpower, and special legal powers and favorable tax treatment. Peter's son, Roswell Colt, led the effort to acquire outstanding shares. He envisioned a transformed SUM. The revised model offered industrial sites, waterpower, and mill space to foster privately owned businesses. Within a decade, a number of mills were constructed along a raceway system. Roswell Colt emerged as Paterson's leading citizen and his home, Roswell House, was the grandest home in the city. It was located on a hill that was considered by Pierre L'Enfant as the site of a grand public building. (Courtesy of the Paterson Museum, Paterson, New Jersey.)

By the 1830s, there were over 20 cotton mills of various sizes using the power of the raceway system. Other industries grew in Paterson's industrial district, including paper, metalworks, and machinery manufacturing. This area was the location of the factory where Peter Colt's nephew Samuel Colt developed the patent revolver. (Both, courtesy of the Paterson Museum, Paterson, New Jersey.)

To meet the revived demand for Paterson's manufacturing capabilities, the raceways expanded, and the SUM business model adapted to provide land and power on a lease basis. In addition, changes in the tariff laws protected American industries, resulting in pricing advantages for domestically produced fabric. Mills grew along the raceway system. (Both, courtesy of the Paterson Museum, Paterson, New Jersey.)

Along the Morris Canal, Paterson, N. J.

Hello Nellie how are you I will be home a...

After years of planning, in 1836, the Morris Canal connected Paterson with the iron ore–producing areas of western New Jersey and Pennsylvania. In addition, more rail lines connected Paterson to the Hudson River waterfront. Paterson saw the development of foundries that made structural materials and heavy equipment. (Courtesy public domain.)

In 1836, the Morris Canal connected Paterson with the iron ore–producing areas of western New Jersey and Pennsylvania. In addition, rail lines connected Paterson to the Hudson River waterfront and the markets of New York and beyond. During this period, Paterson saw the development of foundries that made structural elements for buildings and bridges, machinery, and iron goods to meet the demand of a growing region. These industries spurred the development of Paterson's emerging industries such locomotive, iron goods, textile machinery, and machine-tool manufacture. (Courtesy of the Paterson Museum, Paterson, New Jersey.)

154

By the late 1830s, Paterson's manufacturing products expanded beyond textiles, realizing the diverse economy that Hamilton envisioned. By the late 1830s, new technology grew out of the local machine shops. By this time, the city had an inventory of mill structures and building sites available with waterpower. The labor force included capable tradesmen. The demand for manufactured products in the growing nation was strong, and the improvements to transportation brought goods and material. Bankers and investors were available to provide the capital a new business required. (Courtesy of the Paterson Museum, Paterson, New Jersey.)

Locomotive manufacturing grew out of the efforts to build early textile mills and related machinery. The skilled mechanics and machinery builders were in Paterson and began expanding their enterprises. Thomas Rogers, the industry leader, was born in Groton, Connecticut, in 1792. After the War of 1812, he came to Paterson to build power looms for the textile industry. By the 1830s, he had a small foundry that was able to forge iron for machinery needed in the mills. In 1836, the New Jersey Railroad and Transportation Company purchased an English locomotive engine and had it sent to Paterson to be assembled. The engine arrived in parts, and Rogers analyzed how it was put together. Before the engine changed hands, Rogers had drawings and patterns of every part of it. By 1837, the locomotive industry was concentrated near the falls on Spruce and Market Streets. These locations were powered by the raceway system. Over the coming years, Rogers was Paterson's largest employer and wealthiest citizen. (Courtesy of the Paterson Museum, Paterson, New Jersey.)

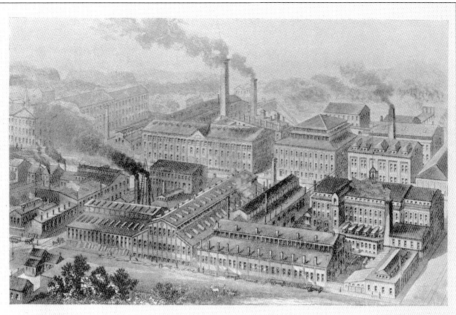

ROGERS LOCOMOTIVE COMPANY.

Address, Paterson, N. J. or 44 Exchange Place, New York.

⸺BUILDERS OF⸺

Locomotive Engines and Tenders of Every Description.

R. S. HUGHES, PRESIDENT.　　　G. E. HANNAH, TREASURER.
G. H. LONGBOTTOM, SECRETARY.　　REUBEN WELLS, SUPERINTENDENT.

The Rogers Locomotive Works grew to occupy both sides of Spruce Street in the Great Falls district (some Rogers buildings survive today; one is occupied by the Paterson Museum). Other locomotive manufacturers developed in Paterson as well, mostly in the same general area of the raceway system. Danforth Locomotive and Machine Company was also a highly regarded manufacturer, and engine No. 387 is an example of its products. (Both, courtesy of the Paterson Museum, Paterson, New Jersey.)

From 1837 to 1900, Rogers produced 5,654 locomotives, with peak production years in the 1870s. In the Civil War years and beyond, Paterson locomotives were among the finest available and had a major role in connecting the nation—a Paterson locomotive helped complete the transcontinental railway and was at the golden spike ceremony in Promontory Point, Utah, in 1869. Paterson locomotives had an international market and were indispensable in building the infrastructure of Peru and the Panama Canal. (Courtesy of the Library of Congress.)

The area surrounding the locomotive plants became highly congested. Logistics were increasingly difficult and inefficient because the factories were not on the rail line. Locomotives were brought through the city streets to the rail lines on horse-drawn trolleys. The process often resulted in traffic shutdowns. The manufacturing of locomotives came to an end around 1900, when Rogers stopped taking new orders. The industry consolidated outside of Paterson. However, locomotives remain a milestone in Paterson's development. (Courtesy of the Paterson Museum, Paterson, New Jersey.)

The growth of heavy industry in Paterson required energy infrastructure and a capable workforce. These photographs show the James Wilson & Son Coal Yard on the side of a railroad line and the type of workforce needed to construct complex machinery like locomotives and other heavy equipment. (Both, courtesy of the Paterson Museum, Paterson, New Jersey.)

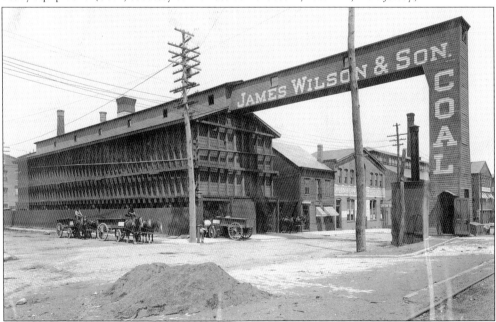

Two

THE SILK INDUSTRY ARRIVES

The Paterson silk industry took shape beginning in 1840, when John Ryle took over operations of a failed silk spinning operation from Christopher Colt in the upper floors of the Colt Gun Mill. This same mill was the birthplace of the Colt revolver in 1837. John Ryle was from Macclesfield, a town in northwestern England, where he had worked in the silk industry. Ryle started up the Paterson plant producing "sewing silk," a spooled silk used in the new sewing machines produced by Isaac Singer. (Courtesy of the Paterson Museum, Paterson, New Jersey.)

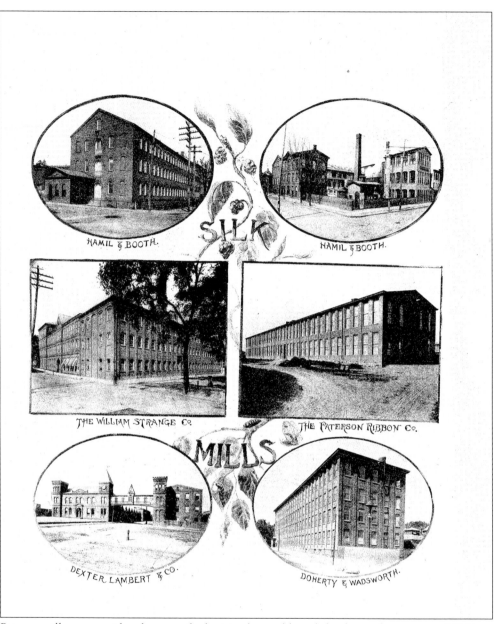

Paterson silk was considered among the best in the world, and the demand was strong. Within a matter of years, just about all of the older cotton mills were repurposed, and new efficient buildings were constructed to meet demand. The industry responded with large, fully integrated silk mills that employed hundreds of workers. In their day, these were among the most efficient silk mills in the world. These mills were designed for the complex process of silk production. All of the processes—winding, cleaning, doubling, twisting, rewinding, and reeling—were under one roof. The most competitive of the Paterson mills contained the full range of processes. Several mills were designed exclusively for silk production: Hamil and Booth (two mills); the William Strange Mill; Paterson Ribbon Company; Dexter, Lambert and Co.; and Doherty and Wadsworth. All grew during the period from 1860 to 1880 when the industry was ascendant. (Courtesy of *History of Paterson and Its Environs*.)

SILK MILL OF THE WILLIAM STRANGE MANUFACTURING COMPANY.

Over time, technologies changed, and mills were less dependent on the use of the raceways to power equipment as steam engines were available and affordable. Access to rail lines was a greater locational benefit, and Paterson had a railway system that served various parts of the city. The William Strange Mill on Beech Street grew in the Civil War era and became one of the most successful silk manufacturers. (Courtesy of *Paterson, New Jersey, Illustrated.*)

SILK MILLS OF DEXTER, LAMBERT & CO.

Mills incorporated the design and architectural style of English textile factories. The mills were generally brick and heavy timber construction and had multiple stories to increase the efficiency of belts and other equipment to run the machinery. The mills often featured large brick pilasters to support the heavy equipment. They had high ceilings and were often U or L shaped and relatively narrow to take advantage of natural light. One of the best known and most successful of the integrated silk mills belonged to Dexter, Lambert and Co. Catholina Lambert became one of the wealthiest citizens in Paterson and the builder of Bella Vista, the city's grandest residence. (Courtesy of *Paterson, New Jersey, Illustrated.*)

In Paterson's ribbon and broad silk weaving factories, the fiber and value of the product defined the work and the relations between the workers and the owners. Owners and weavers were in frequent conflict over productivity, work processes, introduction of new technologies, and work rules. It was a contentious relationship constrained by mutual dependency. Conditions were difficult, and the working day was 10 hours long with a half day on Saturday. The silk threads had to be watched carefully to detect and correct problems, so lighting was critical. New mills were located all over Paterson by the late 19th century and were designed to provide the necessary light and an efficient configuration. There was constant pressure to improve productivity and introduce new technologies. By 1910, approximately 25,000 were employed in 270 Paterson silk mills and another 10,000 in 75 silk dyeing and printing establishments. (Courtesy of the Paterson Museum, Paterson, New Jersey.)

Immigrant labor was a critical component of the silk industry. In England, the 1860 Anglo-French trade treaty opened England's silk market to French goods, hurting the English silk industry. Macclesfield became uncompetitive, and skilled silk workers relocated to Paterson where they were the largest initial workforce. In the coming decades, immigrant workers from Holland, Italy, Poland, Russia, Sweden, and Switzerland filled the ranks of Paterson's workforce. (Both, courtesy of the Paterson Museum, Paterson, New Jersey.)

SILK MILL OF DOHERTY & WADSWORTH.

The introduction of steam power in 1859 changed the dependence of the mills on the raceway system. While the older mills remained on the raceway system, newer ones included self-contained steam-powered plants that freed them to locate elsewhere. The original Doherty and Watson Mill was located along the middle raceway and had five levels of manufacturing with a monitor extending the roofline to bring in natural light. (Courtesy of *Paterson, New Jersey, Illustrated*.)

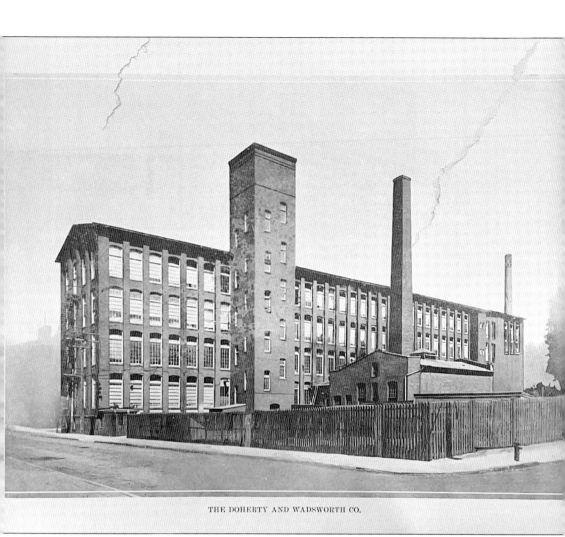

THE DOHERTY AND WADSWORTH CO.

The Doherty and Watson plant shows the mill design with a dedicated steam plant and elaborate stair tower to assist the movement of goods and workers to the upper levels. (Courtesy of *Paterson, New Jersey, Illustrated.*)

SPRUCE STREET MILL OF THE BARBOUR FLAX SPINNING COMPANY.

Not all of the textile mills manufactured silk. Paterson was the home of the Barbour Flax Spinning Company, a leading producer of industrial linen thread. The Barbour brothers arrived in Paterson in 1864 and were part of a family-owned enterprise based in Northern Ireland. The firm started in a mill on Spruce Street and expanded to Grand Street to meet growing demand. Under the leadership of Col. William Barbour, the family-owned firm was an innovator in a range of businesses and leading civic leaders. (Courtesy of *Paterson, New Jersey, Illustrated*.)

The Barbours were familiar with a European model of factory towns and were one of the only firms to offer housing to their workforce. There were several residential complexes for Barbour workers. Company life went beyond the factory. The photograph above shows the members of the Barbour Grand Street baseball team, one of several factory-based teams that played in Paterson's parks and ball fields. (Courtesy of the Paterson Museum, Paterson, New Jersey.)

Dyehouses were located along the Passaic River and grew in parallel with textile manufacturing in the city. The dyehouses tended to be low, long buildings. Conditions were hot and wet, and the work was difficult and dangerous. Dyehouses were in Paterson because of the availability of water, an available workforce, and the lack of environmental regulations. At its peak, the industry employed approximately 10,000 workers. (Both, courtesy of the Paterson Museum, Paterson, New Jersey.)

I.W.W. MEET... ...F THE PATERSON STRIKERS
HELD AT HALEDON, N.J. MAY, 1913

It was widely said that the great 1913 Silk Strike put an end to Paterson's silk industry. The actual story is more complicated. The competitive pressure on silk manufacturers and the conflict between skilled silk weavers and other workers was a continuous issue. The most climactic took place in 1913 with a six-month strike of more than 20,000 silk workers. Silk workers rallied outside of Paterson in nearby Haledon at the home of a striker shown here. The 1913 strike was hard fought and attracted national attention. There were several confrontations between the police and strikers. The cause attracted the intellectuals in Greenwich Village, and on June 7, 1913, the workers staged a pageant in Madison Square Garden that highlighted their cause. The strike ended with no clear winners and a weakened silk industry. (Courtesy of the Paterson Museum, Paterson, New Jersey.)

During this period, the city continued attempts to maintain and attract industry. The hydroelectric plant at the site of the Great Falls was a major innovation in providing power in Paterson. Under the terms of the older agreements, the SUM had an obligation to provide power to the mill sites, and that responsibility was mitigated by diversion of water away from the raceways. To meet this requirement, the SUM introduced hydroelectric and steam plants at the falls. The hydroelectric building remains an iconic element at the Great Falls site. (Courtesy of the Paterson Museum, Paterson, New Jersey.)

Watson Machinery was another major manufacturer of industrial materials and machinery. The company evolved from its beginnings as a foundry that produced bridges and architectural components. Its products are found in the Metropolitan Museum of Art and the Museum of Natural History in Manhattan. Watson was an innovator and early in the 20th century experimented in automobile production. This photograph was taken outside of the Watson factory and shows automobiles being shipped by train cars. (Courtesy of the Paterson Museum, Paterson, New Jersey.)

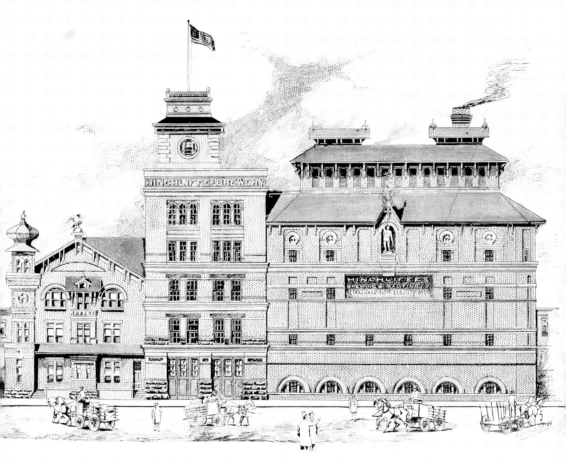

THE HINCHLIFFE BREWERY.

Paterson was the third-largest regional brewing center after New York City and Newark. In 1870–1871, there were eight breweries in Paterson, with the two largest operations being those of Graham & Post at the corner of Hamburg and Matlock Streets and Shaw, Hinchliffe & Company at Governor and Ann Streets. Hinchliffe was established in 1867 as Eagle Brewery. Until the advent of mechanical refrigeration in the 1890s, lager houses were cooled with natural ice harvested from lakes in winter and stored for use in summer. The Hinchliffe Brewery relied on steam power to heat the wort. Portions of the Hinchliffe Brewery building remain, exhibiting the ornate architectural embellishments of the period. Members of the Hinchliffe family became active in local politics and served in important public offices. (Courtesy of *Paterson, New Jersey, Illustrated*.)

Paterson had German-style breweries as well, and there was a sizable settlement of German immigrants in the city. The Braun Brewery and Katz Bros. Brewery were substantial enterprises that were successful in their day. Paterson was home to five prominent regional brewing firms. (Both, courtesy of the Paterson Museum, Paterson, New Jersey.)

Three

RESIDENTIAL DEVELOPMENT

Residential development in Paterson started modestly. The first Europeans in the area were Dutch, who were the earliest settlers. Interest in the area around the Great Falls began in 1695, and the most significant impact was the plan for the city known as the Boght Patent in 1714. This plan laid out parcels and established a development pattern and some streets. Homes built in the early 19th century by Dutch homesteaders were simple and functional. (Courtesy of the Paterson Museum, Paterson, New Jersey.)

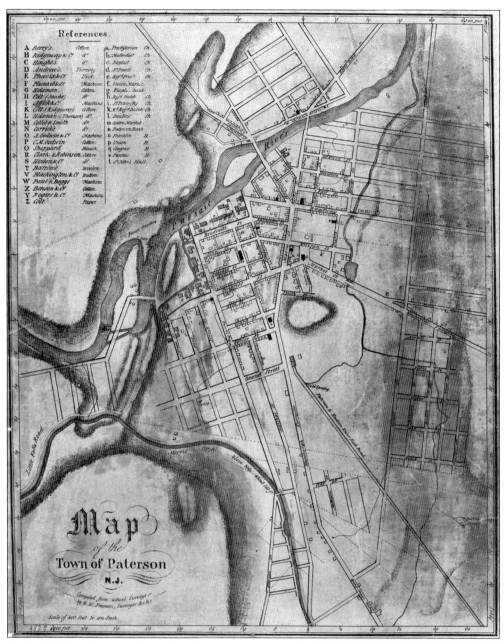

As the SUM took root in the early 19th century, most of the housing was interspersed in the area. Housing locations are shown in this map from 1833 by surveyor U.W. Freeman. Land was relatively cheap and plentiful, which allowed development to fill in quickly. Unlike the New England model, company housing was not typically provided. In the early years, mill owners and workers lived in close proximity to each other. (Courtesy of the Paterson Museum, Paterson, New Jersey.)

Residential neighborhoods grew, and the first real community in Paterson was an area south of the falls that came to be known as the Dublin neighborhood. It contained a range of homes of various types. The name reportedly reflected the origins of the builders of the raceway system who settled in the area. Dublin became a defining neighborhood in Paterson and over the decades has been home to a variety of ethnic groups arriving in the city. Mobility has been a part of the Paterson housing pattern; however, over many generations, Dublin has remained the quintessential Paterson working-class neighborhood. (Courtesy of the Paterson Museum, Paterson, New Jersey.)

As a result of Paterson's success in the mid-19th century, more elaborate and prosperous neighborhoods emerged. The mill owners and professionals became prosperous as the city grew and sought better housing reflecting that prosperity. In short order, Paterson became a showcase for the architectural styles and fashions of the day. Among the toniest residential neighborhoods was one along Van Houten and Colt Streets in what is currently downtown. This tree-lined neighborhood developed in the 1840s and 1850s with well-designed Federal-style buildings like those shown here. These were the homes of the city's newly growing upper and middle classes. (Left, courtesy of the Paterson Museum, Paterson, New Jersey; below, courtesy of *Paterson, New Jersey, Illustrated*.)

VIEW ON ELLISON STREET EAST OF COLT STREET.

RESIDENCE OF HON. GARRET A. HOBART.

The introduction of trolley lines along Broadway and Park Avenue led to the development of fashionable residential neighborhoods along those streets in the Eastside of Paterson. The most striking and substantial of the grand new homes were built along Broadway. The detailed Victorian architecture made a statement about the success and importance of the residents. An example of the emerging prosperity was the home of Garret A. Hobart. He was the leading attorney in the city and an important political leader. Hobart became prominent in the Republican Party's leadership. He ultimately became part of the national ticket and was elected vice president of the United States under William A. McKinley. Hobart died in office. Had he lived, he would have been in line to serve as president when McKinley was assassinated. (Courtesy of the Paterson Museum, Paterson, New Jersey.)

The changing architectural fashions in the mid- to late 19th century created a striking display of building types and styles along Broadway. Simple home designs evolved into ornate Victorian fashion. The early Victorian styles here show the growing interest in Italianate designs popularized in magazines and pattern books. Paterson during its most prosperous period reflected the style of the time and featured decorated and colorful Victorian designs with elaborate features and picturesque facades. (Both, courtesy of the Paterson Museum, Paterson, New Jersey.)

The grand homes reflect the lifestyle of the well-to-do. These included an array of professional and business leaders. William Nelson, whose home is shown at right, was an attorney and title company owner. Nelson was the prolific author of many books and articles about Paterson history that remain an indispensable window into the life of the city. The Cadmus family was a distinguished Paterson family of Dutch descent who were among the city's earliest residents. (Both, courtesy of *Paterson, New Jersey, Illustrated*.)

RESIDENCE OF MR. WILLIAM NELSON.

RESIDENCE OF MR. CORNELIUS A. CADMUS.

45

Silk mill owners who became especially affluent were ready to make a statement about their importance. Jacob Horandt was a Swiss-born silk manufacturer prominent in local circles. Horandt & Son was a major silk manufacturer, and the Horandt house (above) was among the most ornate in the city. One of the giants of the Paterson silk industry was William Strange, whose mill was among the first and most important integrated silk mills in the city. As his elaborate house below indicates, he was one of the most successful silk manufacturers in the city. (Both, courtesy of *Paterson, New Jersey, Illustrated*.)

RESIDENCE OF MR. HENRY B. CROSBY.

The Crosby residence on Broadway, near Straight Street, attracted the wealthy residents of the city and became the epicenter of Victorian glory in Paterson. According to a news article in 1890, "Mr. Crosby's residence on Broadway is one of the landmarks of the city; although now situated in the very heart of Paterson, the spot where it stands was, when he purchased and began the erection of the building, a cornfield. Its architecture was different from that of any of the houses which had been erected in the city and people came many miles to see the structure in which Mr. Crosby proposed to live." This residence later became the Miriam Barnert Dispensary, the first home of what would become the Barnert Hospital. (Courtesy of *Paterson, New Jersey, Illustrated.*)

RESIDENCE OF MR. HENRY DOHERTY.

RESIDENCE OF MR. JAMES A. MORRISSE.

These are the homes of two successful business owners in Paterson. Henry Doherty was a silk weaver who emigrated from Macclesfield, England. After working in the Paterson mills for a decade, he partnered with Joseph Wadsworth, also from Macclesfield, and they invested their savings in establishing a small silk workshop. Their specialties were broad silks, handkerchiefs, and other fancy silks. From these humble beginnings, they had extraordinary success, eventually purchasing larger mills and building factories of their own. They employed almost 1,000 workers by the 1890s. Doherty owned the silk mill that set off the great strike of 1913 when his firm attempted to introduce a "four loom system" that workers rejected. The grand home shown at the bottom was the residence of James A. Morrisse, a businessman, real estate investor, agent, and lender. (Courtesy of *Paterson, New Jersey, Illustrated*.)

William Ryle was a nephew of John Ryle and a prominent silk manufacturer in his own right, with homes in Paterson and New York City. He was president of the Paterson Board of Trade. William Ryle lived in an English-style manor house in Paterson. The home's prominent chimneys created a verticality in the appearance, and the expressive porch broke up volumes of the house. William Ryle married Mary Danforth, the daughter of another leading Patersonian, locomotive manufacturer Charles Danforth. (Courtesy of the Paterson Museum, Paterson, New Jersey.)

RESIDENCE OF MR. ROBERT BARBOUR.

The Barbours were among the most prominent and successful families in the city. Not only were they operating a linen thread business, but the family was also active in the city's banks, utilities, public transport, hospitals, golf and social clubs, and charities. Robert Barbour built this grand Victorian estate on Broadway. (Courtesy of *Paterson, New Jersey, Illustrated*.)

The grandest of the Paterson silk owners' mansions is Belle Vista, located off Valley Street at Garret Mountain, and is known locally as Lambert's Castle. Catholina Lambert made his fortune in Paterson as a silk manufacturer. His home, Belle Vista, has the solidity and presence of old Danish and English castles of the 14th and 15th centuries. The building is constructed of stone, much of which was quarried locally, and its setting on the side of the mountain adds to its imposing presence. It currently serves as the home of the Passaic County Historical Society. (Courtesy of the Paterson Museum, Paterson, New Jersey.)

57

Lambert's success in silk manufacturing enabled him to construct this mansion. In 1896, he added a 35-by-100-foot art gallery wing as well as a 70-foot observation tower (Lambert Tower) with a panoramic view on the cliff and a summerhouse. His art was a major collection of national importance. In 1914, Lambert's company fell into financial distress when the silk strike of 1913 took a toll. Lambert used his estate as collateral to meet the firm's liabilities. As the two-year deadline for repayment approached, Lambert was forced to sell part of the art collection. An auction took place in February 1916, and the forced sale impacted its ultimate return. The house is now part of Passaic County's park system and is open to the public. (Both, courtesy of the Paterson Museum, Paterson, New Jersey.)

Not all Patersonians lived in castles and mansions. The poor were often relegated to inadequate conditions in locations prone to flooding. Paterson was a city where home ownership could be an opportunity to build family equity or where renters relied on private landlords. Consequently, Paterson has had more than its share of housing problems. The commonly built wood-frame homes were quick to erect but required regular maintenance that was often lacking. (Both, courtesy of the Paterson Museum, Paterson, New Jersey.)

Typically, housing was wood frame, functional, and simply decorated. Two- and three-family houses were the norm even in the more middle-class areas. A common practice was home ownership by family groups who would share the apartments with other family members or act as landlords and lease out units. (Both, courtesy of the Paterson Museum, Paterson, New Jersey.)

Neighborhoods became filled with two- and three-family homes. They still represent the predominant form of housing in the city. Of course, there were other housing types. The apartment building at right is considered the first high-rise multifamily building in Paterson. Located on Straight Street, near Park and Market Streets, this building was a trendsetter for the downtown near the train station and offered what would be called today transit-oriented housing. (Courtesy of the Paterson Museum, Paterson, New Jersey.)

Finally, here is an example of a house built for the growing middle class found throughout the city. Fred Wesley Wentworth was Paterson's leading architect in the late 19th and early 20th centuries. He settled in Paterson only five years after graduating from Dartmouth College, and he built this home in 1892 on East Twenty-Fifth Street off Broadway. It reflects the middle-class aspirations of the growing Eastside of the city. (Courtesy of the Paterson Museum, Paterson, New Jersey.)

Dozens of local neighborhood centers grew up throughout the city with storefronts on the ground level and apartments on the upper floors. The ground-floor uses often reflected the ethnic makeup of the area. These images are typical of what was found in the neighborhoods. The above image shows a storefront with a political club. Below, proud workers at the Swiss Bakery line up for a photograph. Paterson had a significant Swiss community who arrived to work in the silk industry, and Swiss community festivals were often held in the downtown area. (Both, courtesy of the Paterson Museum, Paterson, New Jersey.)

Four

HOUSES OF WORSHIP

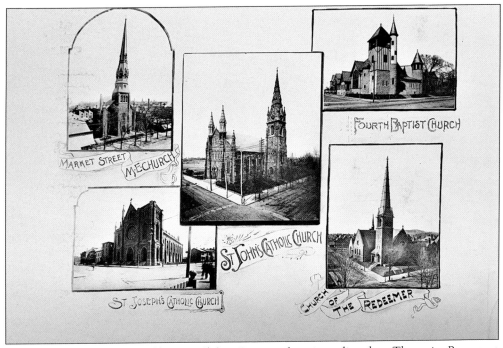

Churches were an indispensable part of life in Paterson from its earliest days. The major Protestant denominations arrived in the early 19th century, and the SUM provided land for minimal consideration. First Presbyterian Church was formed in 1814; other denominations followed. By the end of the 1840s, most of the major church denominations had a presence in the city. European immigrant communities also arrived, establishing houses of worship for English, Swiss, Dutch, German, Irish, Jewish, and Swedish citizens. The African American community also had its churches. The buildings in the city were an expression of the growing financial capacity of recently arrived communities. The trend in architectural designs in the early 1800s were reminiscent of European churches. The most influential design at this time was Trinity Church in lower Manhattan, designed by Richard Upjohn in 1848. The New York church undoubtedly influenced church designs throughout the region, including Paterson. (Courtesy of *History of Paterson and Its Environs*.)

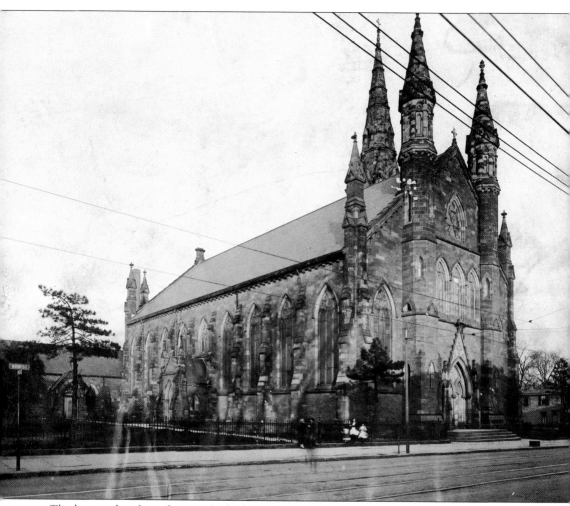

The largest church in the city, Cathedral of St. John the Baptist, was built on a portion of land carved out from Roswell Colt's estate. The Catholic community engaged P.C. Kiely, a prominent church architect who also designed the cathedrals in Boston, Providence, and Chicago, to design a new neo-Gothic church. The brownstone used for St. John's was quarried in Little Falls, brought to Paterson on the Morris Canal, and dressed on the construction site. Like medieval cathedrals, St. John's was built by labor provided by members of the parish. It took around 30 years to build and remains a center of Catholic life to the present. (Courtesy of the Paterson Museum, Paterson, New Jersey.)

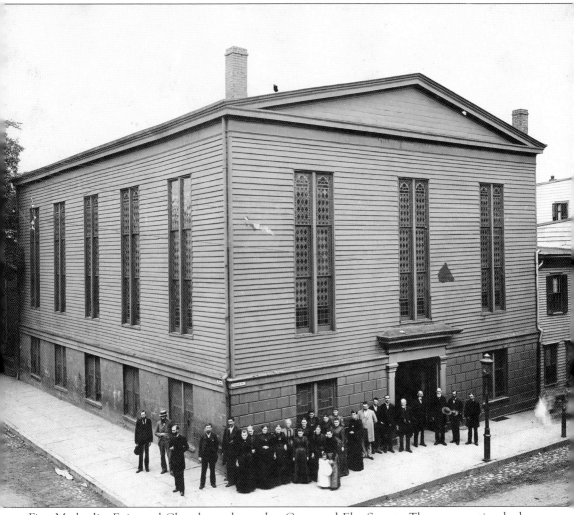

First Methodist Episcopal Church was located at Cross and Elm Streets. The congregation had its origins going back to 1805, when circuit riders would preach in a mill building. This building, constructed in 1836, shows church design at its most basic and austere. There were three Methodist Episcopal congregations, and they decided to consolidate. This congregation merged with Market Steet Methodist Episcopal Church. (Courtesy of the Paterson Museum, Paterson, New Jersey.)

Market Street Methodist Episcopal Church was the third church of this denomination and was an outgrowth of the Cross Street congregation. This handsome building was completed in 1871 when the spire was added. It became the leading church of the denomination when the Cross Street congregation merged into this congregation in 1904. The building was known as "the Beehive of Methodism." It is no longer standing. (Courtesy of the Paterson Museum, Paterson, New Jersey.)

Immigrant Dutch communities in northern New Jersey grew quickly between 1856 and 1869. As a result, five Dutch congregations were formed, including in the Paterson community. The First Dutch Reformed Church at Hamilton Avenue was founded in 1755. Members erected a church on land belonging to Henry Brockholst on Water and Matlock Streets. This building is the grandest of the Dutch churches. (Courtesy of the Paterson Museum, Paterson, New Jersey.)

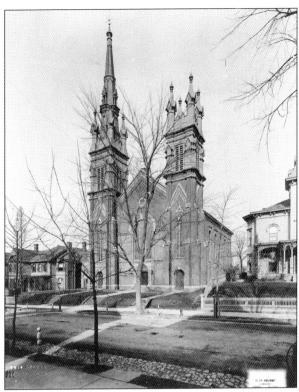

The Christian Science church was constructed in 1914 on the corner of Fair and Auburn Streets. (Courtesy of the Paterson Museum, Paterson, New Jersey.)

First Presbyterian Church is among the oldest churches in the city of Paterson and is located at the corner of Ward and Main Streets. The First Presbyterian Society was formed on August 19, 1813. The first pastor was the Reverend Samuel Fisher. The property for the new church was donated by the SUM. The original church on this site was made of brick, and being one of the first brick buildings in town, it became known as the "Brick Church." That building was destroyed in 1850. The building shown here was promptly constructed and dedicated in 1852. (Courtesy of the Paterson Museum, Paterson, New Jersey.)

This view of Broadway facing east from Straight Street gives a striking image of two houses of worship. St. Mark's Protestant Episcopal Church is on the left. The building at right is the oldest Jewish congregation in Paterson, Congregation Bnai Jeshrun (known as the "Barnert Temple"). Take note of the streetcar heading toward downtown from the city's Eastside. The Barnert Temple was founded in 1848 by a small German Jewish community, which originally met in smaller facilities. The synagogue shown here was designed in a Moorish style by New York architect John Post in 1899. The land was donated by mill owner and civic leader Nathan Barnert. The building remained the home of the congregation until 1965, when a new structure was constructed on Wall Avenue and Fourteenth Avenue on the Eastside of Paterson. (Courtesy of the Jewish Historical Society of Northern New Jersey.)

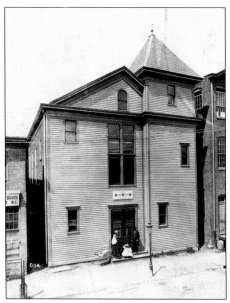

First African Methodist Episcopal Zion Church is the oldest Black church in Paterson and Passaic County. Founded in 1834, the church reported in 1835 that it had 22 members and that the Reverend William Serrington was the pastor in charge. Located on the north side of Godwin Street, the church was initially known as the Godwin Street AME Zion Church. Congregants of this church played an important role in the city's affairs over the decades. (Courtesy of the Paterson Museum, Paterson, New Jersey.)

St. Joseph's Church was founded in 1875 to serve the growing population of Catholics in Paterson. The parish grew quickly and became one of the largest congregations in the city. The devastating fire of February 1902 spread up Market Street to the Sandy Hill Park area and gutted St. Joseph's Church. The parish rallied to rebuild. Work got underway quickly, and the church was rebuilt and evolved into a vibrant parish church with schools and other social facilities. (Courtesy of the Paterson Museum, Paterson, New Jersey.)

Five

THE GROWTH OF THE COMMERCIAL DOWNTOWN

Over time, Paterson evolved from a sleepy village to a vibrant and successful commercial center. As the area developed, Paterson became the retail, banking, governmental, and entertainment core of the region and relied on a strong local system of transportation that linked the city to the adjoining neighborhoods and communities. This view of Main Street, looking south toward Garret Mountain, shows the city in the mid-1800s. Main Street grew rapidly over the mid- to late 19th century, reinventing itself multiple times. This photograph has a primitive feel to it, and Paterson was a frontier town in its earliest years. The earliest merchants served the local agricultural providers, and it was fairly common for the shops to serve farmers, machinists, and small-scale manufacturing. (Courtesy of the Paterson Museum, Paterson, New Jersey.)

These images show an active market for food, commodities, and necessities as well as animal feed, industrial equipment, and distribution. The simple and straightforward buildings that housed these services were functional and largely unadorned. (Both, courtesy of the Paterson Museum, Paterson, New Jersey.)

As Paterson's economy matured in the later years of the 19th century, the commercial downtown became more sophisticated and elaborate. These commercial buildings near Main Street reflect the maturity of Paterson's architecture. Downtown Paterson was the place to go for all kinds of retail and food stores. This retail building at right is all decked out for the Fourth of July. The unadorned building style below shows the desire for practical construction that could be decorated effectively for holidays. (Both, courtesy of the Paterson Museum, Paterson, New Jersey.)

This classic Victorian structure was the home to Lankering Cigars, an establishment that thrived in Paterson into the late 20th century. This original location featured a cigar store Indian and festive bunting. The celebration may have been Paterson's centennial, and the banner includes a woven portrait of Alexander Hamilton. (Courtesy of the Paterson Museum, Paterson, New Jersey.)

8

Market Street was originally known as Congress Street, and the four-story building shown here was known as Congress Hall, the heart of the city's business center. This photograph was taken before the Paterson City Hall was constructed, and St. Paul's Episcopal Church, which was originally on the site, is visible in the photograph. (Courtesy of the Paterson Museum, Paterson, New Jersey.)

In the early 1890s, Congress Hall was replaced by an elaborate masonry high-rise that was the home of the Paterson Institute for Savings. The bank grew based on the area's residential growth and was the leading provider of mortgages in the local market. The building is an elaborate Italian Beaux-Arts Romanesque design with terra-cotta features. Note the highly stylized English-style Victorian building immediately to the north of the new structure. In 1902, a devastating fire destroyed a large portion of downtown Paterson. The Great Fire remains the largest fire in New Jersey history and truly shaped the downtown that developed and remains today. (Courtesy of the Paterson Museum, Paterson, New Jersey.)

As the downtown grew quickly in the late 19th century, its infrastructure struggled to keep up with the city's growth. The web of overhead wires and the wood-frame construction of most of the downtown show the need for expediency in building the city. All were perfect fuel that ultimately contributed to the greatest fire in New Jersey history in 1902. A majority of the buildings in this photograph were destroyed in the conflagration. The fire would have spread farther were it not for the firestop of masonry provided by the Paterson Institution for Savings, which kept the fire from travelling south and destroying even more property. (Courtesy of the Paterson Museum, Paterson, New Jersey.)

This view shows the Paterson Institution for Savings in the years after the fire. The area was evolving, with the new city hall seen in the background replacing a church that had been there previously. The Schoonmakers store on the left replaced the Victorian building after the fire and stood for approximately 20 years until it was replaced by a larger commercial structure. (Courtesy of the Paterson Museum, Paterson, New Jersey.)

The post-fire years were the most prosperous for this location. The corner of Main and Market Streets was one of the most active intersections in the city. The Schoonmakers store was replaced by a three-story building and, because of the location's importance, the skyscraper shown here was constructed in the late 1910s. The introduction of steel framing allowed the large open facade. This Chicago-style modern commercial building was designed by Paterson's architect, Fred Wesley Wentworth. It is still standing on Main Steet and remains a display of architectural influences of the early 20th century. (Courtesy of the Paterson Museum, Paterson, New Jersey.)

The area near Broadway and Washington Street is another study of changes in the cityscape of Paterson during the period of the city's greatest growth. The handsome Second Empire commercial building known as Washington Hall was constructed as the era opened in the 1860s. The first floor was retail, including ice cream and housewares, while the second floor was the largest hall in town. The surrounding buildings were the most basic commercial structures imaginable. The building with the sign for oysters and dining was a stop in the antebellum years for Paterson's Underground Railroad. (Courtesy of the Paterson Museum, Paterson, New Jersey.)

This view of Broadway is from the 1870s. Tracks for horse-drawn trolleys can be seen in the foreground. (Courtesy of the Paterson Museum, Paterson, New Jersey.)

When the Barnum circus arrived in Paterson, the elephants paraded along Broadway; Washington Hall framed their route. News articles from the period confirm that the circus was in Paterson on April 27, 1895, and offered a complete performance with all the acts appearing at a racetrack in Clifton. One can only imagine the excitement that a circus parade with a herd of elephants must have caused as they made their way through the heart of the young city. (Courtesy of the Paterson Museum, Paterson, New Jersey.)

A fire destroyed Washington Hall, and it was replaced with this larger commercial design. The adjoining building with a tower was the home of the *Paterson Morning Call*, one of several daily newspapers that served Paterson during this period. (Courtesy of the Paterson Museum, Paterson, New Jersey.)

At a time when Paterson was a major center for industrial machinery design and manufacture, local firms and mechanics needed their tools. This area in downtown became home to suppliers of tools, parts, and equipment. Cleveland Hardware was among the largest. (Courtesy of the Paterson Museum, Paterson, New Jersey.)

By the early part of the 20th century, Washington Street had become the major in-town food market. The streets were lined with small vegetable vendors, live poultry markets, fruit and nuts stores, and the like. Here is the scene around 1920 showing the new use. Note that the tower of the Morning Call building has been removed to give the building a more contemporary look. (Courtesy of the Paterson Museum, Paterson, New Jersey.)

Six

THE HEART OF THE CITY

As part of the centennial celebration of the city's founding, Paterson commissioned the design and construction of a signature building—its new city hall. Leading architectural firms competed, and the winning design was from the prominent firm of Carriere and Hastings. It was only fitting that the Lyon of America would have a city hall that drew inspiration from France's "Silk City." The Paterson City Hall Tower is directly derived from its French counterpart, the Hotel de Ville in Lyon. As is only appropriate, the surrounding buildings that grew up during this period and the professional offices serving a prosperous and growing city echoed the French design theme. (Courtesy of the Paterson Museum, Paterson, New Jersey.)

At the new heart of Paterson, the city hall and the Second National Bank recall the buildings of France. These were two of the grandest buildings downtown. Local critics favored the Second National Bank to the new city hall. On June 6, 1895, before the fire, the *Paterson Evening News* wrote, "Anybody who compares the Second National bank architecturally with our botched and bangled new city hall will be glad that no Paterson man is responsible for such an architectural atrocity. Imported talent is welcome to all the glory of its unadorned ugliness." (Courtesy of the Paterson Museum, Paterson, New Jersey.)

The Second National Bank was built in the 1890s in an elaborate Beaux-Arts style. The elaborate mansard roof and chimneys framed City Hall Plaza. The building is still standing, although portions of the mansard roof have been removed. (Courtesy of the Paterson Museum, Paterson, New Jersey.)

Several commercial buildings adjacent to the city hall also recall French architectural character and the Beaux-Arts influence that was so popular at the turn of the 20th century. Market Street was lined with offices and ground-floor retail establishments. The collection of buildings gave character to and helped form Paterson's center of town. (Courtesy of the Paterson Museum, Paterson, New Jersey.)

The fire of 1902 caused extensive damage. Here, the scorched city hall is seen next to the devastated Second National Bank building with the damaged mansard roof. While the property loss to the downtown was enormous, the industrial areas were untouched, and the city had the resources to get back to work quickly. The rebuilding effort began within months, and many of the new structures were of distinctive design. In fact, the downtown core of Paterson today is largely the buildings that were constructed in the post-fire era, making Paterson a showcase for early-20th-century architecture. (Both, courtesy of the Paterson Museum, Paterson, New Jersey.)

The Colt Building, constructed shortly after the fire, is located directly across from city hall on Ellison Street and Colt Street. The building was designed for the city's most prominent professionals and featured high ceilings and elaborate interiors. The architect was Alexander Mackintosh, best known for the design of the Rhinelander Mansion on Madison Avenue and East Seventy-ninth Street, currently known as the Ralph Lauren Building. (Courtesy of the Paterson Museum, Paterson, New Jersey.)

The Silk City Trust Company on Market Street is a six-story, three-bay, granite Beaux-Arts classicized building. It was constructed in 1905. The building has block pilasters and a heavily rusticated granite surface over the entire facade. It is near city hall on Market Street and is the tallest masonry building in the city. The structure is estimated to be six feet thick at the base and is among the most monumental buildings in downtown Paterson. It remains one of the city's significant commercial structures. (Courtesy of the Paterson Museum, Paterson, New Jersey.)

The Hamilton Savings Bank was the major banking center for the silk industry in Paterson. The front streetscape was like the famed buttonwood tree of Wall Street—the place where buyers and sellers, owners and weavers, and lenders and borrowers would meet to transact business. The bank's collapse in the Great Depression marked additional damage to the remaining silk industry. Sadly, the facade was modernized in the 1950s. (Both, courtesy of the Paterson Museum, Paterson, New Jersey.)

The visual of the Greek temples dedicated to banking was a popular architectural form during this era. With the pantheon located across the street at the Hamilton Trust Company, the Second National Bank addition provided an imposing granite facade for its expansion from the French-style, Beaux-Arts structure next door. This building remains a fixture on Market Street, although it is no longer used for banking. It is notable for its colossal, fluted Doric columns; bronze medallions; and floral plaques. (Courtesy of the Paterson Museum, Paterson, New Jersey.)

The L'Enfant Building was home to the German American Bank; it is credited to architect Alexander Mackintosh. As frequently happened during the First World War, organizations that were associated with all things German changed their name to disassociate with their wartime foe. The German American Bank became the Franklin Bank. This building is still standing and has housed some memorable Paterson businesses. (Courtesy of the Paterson Museum, Paterson, New Jersey.)

In the early 20th century, well-capitalized businessmen joined together to form local commercial banks. Paterson had a variety of local banks to meet lending opportunities. Citizens Trust Co. was one of the new banks, founded in 1901, and its new headquarters opened after the fire. The bank thrived during the post-fire building boom. Citizens offered a wide range of lending services for smaller businesses and families. Professional offices, including those of Fred Wesley Wentworth, filled the upper floors. (Courtesy of the Paterson Museum, Paterson, New Jersey.)

In a few brief years following the Great Fire of 1902, virtually all of Ellison Street behind city hall was brought back to life. Fred Wesley Wentworth was the most accomplished and capable of the local architects and was given a variety of commissions to rebuild the city. This building was constructed for the *Paterson Evening News*, which occupied the structure until the 1960s. It has a romantic quality to it, with its heavily ornamented roofline and entryway. The building has been demolished. (Courtesy of the Paterson Museum, Paterson, New Jersey.)

This picture reflects the resilience and dynamism of Paterson during this era. The view is from City Hall Plaza in 1923, about 20 years after the Great Fire. The downtown of the city is largely rebuilt and functioning at a high level of design and activity. What is striking is that this photograph was taken about 60 years from the time the city started to find its economic strength. Within two generations, a mature city had evolved. (Courtesy of the Paterson Museum, Paterson, New Jersey.)

This photograph of Ellison Street behind Paterson City Hall was taken around 1910. Considering that Paterson's growth really began in the Civil War era, it was still a very young city and acquired maturity way beyond its years. The downtown had seen several iterations by this time, and these buildings formed an urban ensemble that largely remains to the current date. (Courtesy of the Paterson Museum, Paterson, New Jersey.)

City Hall Plaza was and remains to this day the ceremonial heart of the city. It is a place where candidates come to campaign, parades mark special anniversaries, and crowds gather at the end of conflicts or to protest their concerns. These images show how this area has served as the center of the city for many years and is still part of the Paterson identity. (Both, courtesy of the Paterson Museum, Paterson, New Jersey.)

In the late 19th century, nearly every city in America had a major building project constructed by the federal government. It was a deliberate display of the federal government's power and influence. In Paterson, that building was a new post office constructed in a Dutch style based on the Haarlem Bourse. The site was formerly the home of Roswell Colt, which was demolished and the hill leveled. In the following years, the new post office and county court complex were constructed on the site to form the center of governmental buildings. This photograph shows the beginning of the construction. (Courtesy of the Passiac County Historical Society.)

This was an era when landmark customhouses, federal buildings, and post offices were constructed throughout the country by the federal government. The US Treasury Department had a staff of architects for any assignment. The Paterson Post Office building was designed to recall Flemish architecture and was under the direction of the US Treasury Department. The building was acquired by Passaic County in the 1940s after a new post office opened near the train station. This building remains one of the most distinctive and ornate structures in Paterson. (Courtesy of the Paterson Museum, Paterson, New Jersey.)

In the years following the design and construction of the post office, the county commissioned a new court complex for the adjacent site. Architectural styles had changed, and the City Beautiful Movement had become popular. Classically designed buildings in the Beaux-Arts/City Beautiful style were the fashion. There had been a competition of selected architects for this design, but in the end, the county freeholders ignored the recommendations of the jury and picked the design of Samuel Burrage Reed, a Long Island architect. (Courtesy of the Paterson Museum, Paterson, New Jersey.)

The post office and courthouse are shown nearing completion in the early years of the 20th century. The two buildings, with very divergent styles, make up an unusual cityscape that intrigues visitors. In later years, even more styles of architecture were knitted together to form the governmental complex. These buildings also formed a civic gathering place and are shown below as the location for a concert by the US Navy Band. (Both, courtesy of the Paterson Museum, Paterson, New Jersey.)

Seven

A PORTFOLIO OF BUILDINGS

There is more to Paterson than the statement buildings. This was a working city. The vibrancy of Paterson's downtown in this period is reflected in the quality and design of even its everyday buildings. The city had a striking number of handsome commercial buildings that served local businesses, retailers, and trades. A considerable portion of the commercial buildings supported the industrial trade in the city as well as the farming in rural areas nearby. Muzzy Brothers at 148 Main Street on the corner of Van Houten Street sold everything from manufacturer's supplies to household furnishing and seeds. Their original building was destroyed by the Great Fire of 1902. This building was constructed around 1915. (Courtesy of the Paterson Museum, Paterson, New Jersey.)

The building shown here was George Christie's General Hardware Store at 59 Washington Street at the corner of Fair Street. It was one of the larger providers of industrial materials in the city. (Courtesy of the Paterson Museum, Paterson, New Jersey.)

Another early commercial building was the home of H.W. Mills & Company, a firm catering to the industrial supply market. This simple brick structure with large open windows was similar to the loft buildings found in other early densely populated industrial cities such as New York and Newark. H.W. Mills was located at 59 Washington Street at the corner of Fair Street in an area commonly known as Hardware Row. (Courtesy of the Paterson Museum, Paterson, New Jersey.)

This handsome building was another center for industrial products, such as plows and other heavy equipment. Paterson was the regional center for all kinds of shops and industrial supply firms that brought in commercial interests from throughout the region. (Courtesy of the Paterson Museum, Paterson, New Jersey.)

The emerging public utilities were new on the scene during the late 19th century. Their buildings downtown were well designed and assured the public of their capability and solidity. The Telephone Building, shown here, is the prototypical urban office structure for an institutional owner. (Courtesy of the Paterson Museum, Paterson, New Jersey.)

The Gas and Electric Building, found on Van Houten Street, was a larger version of the urban architecture of the late 19th century. This structure was replaced by a larger building in the post-fire era. (Courtesy of the Paterson Museum, Paterson, New Jersey.)

Paterson commercial activity was so vibrant that second and third floors housed commercial and social centers. The richness of activities enlivened the downtown. The Kitay Building on Main Street has it all: a clothing store, a bakery, and a dentist as well as a pool hall on the top floor. The Scheuer Building on Main Street had an intriguing mix of uses. It started out as a food retailer and evolved over the years. When the photograph below was taken, the building housed a department store on the street front (it became the Paterson branch of Kresge's), a Chinese American restaurant on the second floor, and a veteran's organization on the third floor. (Both, courtesy of the Paterson Museum, Paterson, New Jersey.)

Social clubs were important institutions in the downtown area. The buildings were often the pride of specific communities and often served as locations for gatherings of trade unions, family parties, rallies, and cultural affairs. Among the best known and most important was Helvetia Hall located between the commercial center and the mills. Helvetia Hall was developed by the Swiss community, and others grew in this area serving the needs of the English, Italian, and other ethnicities. Helvetia Hall played a major role as a union setting for many years. (Courtesy of the Paterson Museum, Paterson, New Jersey.)

The photograph above shows the Postal Carrier's Union at Helvetia Hall in October 1911 for its annual celebration and banquet. (Courtesy of the Walter P. Reuther Library, Wayne State University, Heinrichs Photo Co.)

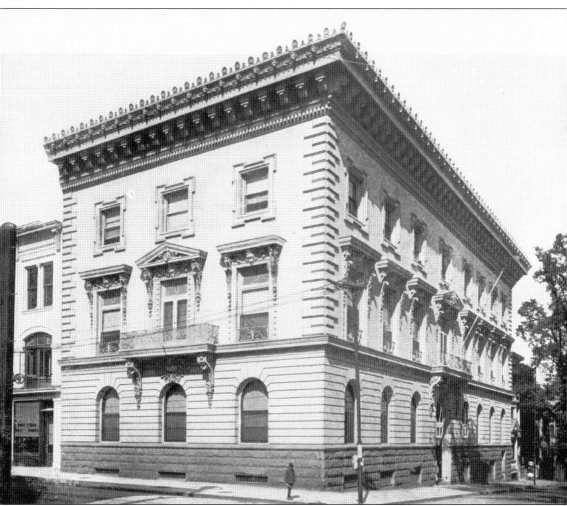

Paterson's business elite had a club of their own, the Hamilton Club. Built on the model of an Italian palazzo, the elegant club housed dining, meeting, and guest room suites for the captains of industry in Paterson. The building was opened in 1897 and was founded by the city's business elite. It was gutted by the Great Fire and rebuilt to its former glory. It proudly stands on the corner of Church and Ellison Streets in the center of the business district, where it remains one of the most distinctive buildings in the city. (Courtesy of the Paterson Museum, Paterson, New Jersey.)

Main Street was a collection of local businesses that offered a range of shops and services. The owner of this store, Jacob Fabian, was born in 1865 in Bavaria. Fabian came to Paterson and operated this successful women's clothing store. After the Great Fire, he rebuilt and then sold the store and planned a new career. Fabian saw an opportunity in motion pictures and opened the Regent Theater in Paterson in 1914. It was a bold move that was a foundation for a very successful theater career. Complimenting his business activities, Fabian became a community leader and an anchor in Paterson's Jewish affairs. (Courtesy of the Paterson Museum, Paterson, New Jersey.)

The years following the 1902 fire set off a building frenzy along Main Street. Paterson opted to rebuild quickly. The National Clothes for Men and Boys building on the corner of Van Houten and Main Streets is an unusual style for Paterson and picks up the Chicago influence of Louis Sullivan with arched windows, dark stone, and organic decoration. (Courtesy of the Paterson Museum, Paterson, New Jersey.)

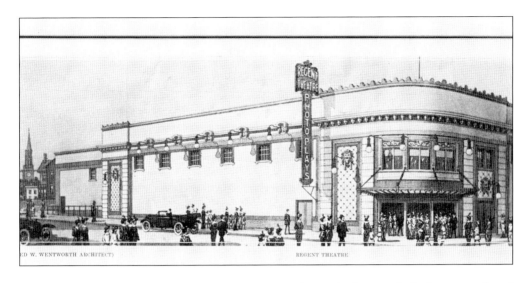

REGENT THEATRE

The first of Jacob Fabian's movie palaces was the Regent Theater, built in 1915. The Regent combined moving picture shows with live entertainment. The biggest names in vaudeville, Broadway, and later radio appeared on its stage. While skeptics doubted that the theater would be successful, it flourished and started Fabian on his way to a movie empire. Paterson became the regional movie theater center with grand movie palaces, most of which were built in the 1920s. (Both, courtesy of the Paterson Museum, Paterson, New Jersey.)

Furniture stores were housed in large warehouse-type buildings that were a major part of the downtown retail scene. Among the largest was the F.C. Van Dyk & Company shop on Main Street. After a fire destroyed the original structure in 1910, a new building was constructed. Another early furniture store was Lockwood Brothers. (Both, courtesy of the Paterson Museum, Paterson, New Jersey.)

Downtown Paterson was the retail place to be in northern New Jersey. Multi-floor buildings had stores at every level. This streetscape from around 1910 shows a variety of buildings housing multiple businesses near the intersection of Main and Market Streets. The city's leading haberdashery was Charles W. Elbow's Men's Clothing Store; other business included L.A. Piaget and Co., Jewelers, Watch Makers and Opticians and Benjamin Kent's Drug Company. (Courtesy of the Paterson Museum, Paterson, New Jersey.)

Charles Elbow's new and modern building was constructed around 1920. The building shows the influence of the Chicago style. Its eclectic facade is finished with terra-cotta, an angled corner, an elaborate terra-cotta cornice, a parapet with decorative panels, and floral studs. The building still stands, although recent modernizations have compromised the design. (Courtesy of the Paterson Museum, Paterson, New Jersey.)

MEYER BROTHERS' DRY GOODS STORE.

The jewels of Paterson's retailing establishments were its two major department stores, Quackenbush's and Meyer Brothers. Both were founded in the late 19th century and came into their own in the post-fire downtown. Meyer Brothers was founded in 1878 and evolved from the Boston Store into the prototypical downtown anchor store that sold just about everything to the middle class. Meyer Brothers remained in business through the 1990s, moving to a suburban location. Sadly, the building was destroyed by a disastrous and fatal fire in November 1991 in which a local fireman lost his life. (Both, courtesy of the Paterson Museum, Paterson, New Jersey.)

The department store rivalry was between Meyer Brothers and Quackenbush's. Both stores had their ardent following. Quackenbush's began as a family-owned business. The Quackenbush family were community leaders and active in civic affairs, supporting parks, schools, and hospitals. The original store burned to the ground in the Great Fire of 1902. The post-fire building was an inviting and attractive store. It was one of the most handsome buildings downtown. Fortunately, it is still standing and continues to operate as a retail center, although only glimpses of its former glory remain. (Courtesy of the Paterson Museum, Paterson, New Jersey.)

Hotels were always a part of Paterson's downtown. As a center of commerce and industry, Paterson had to offer visitors and out-of-towners a comfortable place to stay. A number of hotels met that need, and all were of distinctive design. The US Hotel downtown had a well-regarded restaurant in addition to its rooms. Business meetings were often held there. The unnamed hotel at left offered a grill restaurant and festive decor that was sophisticated and appealing. (Both, courtesy of the Paterson Museum, Paterson, New Jersey.)

The downtown had additional hotels for business travelers. The Hotel Sturmberg was in a handsome building that exuded respectability. During the 1920s, Paterson added the signature hotel for the area, the Alexander Hamilton Hotel. Located on Market and Church Streets, the 210-room hotel had lounges, restaurants, and a ballroom that made it the go-to place in Paterson for 50 years. The hotel was sponsored by the local business community and was adjacent to Jacob Fabian's movie theater and office building. (Both, courtesy of the Paterson Museum, Paterson, New Jersey.)

Paterson's citizens developed the institutions of contemporary life. A prime example is the library. The Paterson Public Library was formed in 1884, when the leading citizens took up the call for a local institution. In 1888, the Danforth family, who were locomotive manufacturers, funded a major new building at the corner of Market and Church Streets. It opened in 1890 and was well stocked with needed reading materials. It was a handsome brownstone building in a late Victorian style. Unfortunately, the Great Fire consumed the entire building and contents, necessitating a new structure. (Both, courtesy of the Paterson Museum, Paterson, New Jersey.)

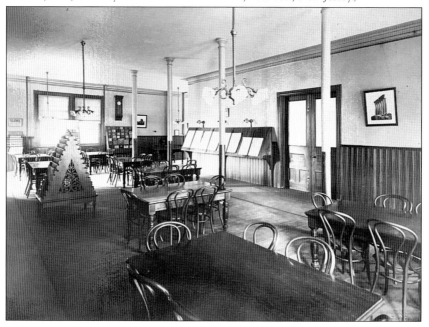

When the fire of February 1902 destroyed the original Danforth library, family member Mary Ryle generously committed to a new, even grander building. It was located among the homes of the city's most well-to-do citizens in what was considered the most fashionable area of the city. (Courtesy of the Paterson Museum, Paterson, New Jersey.)

By October 1903, the new cornerstone was laid. The new, classically designed Danforth Public Library on Broadway was in the center of the city's grandest residential area. The building was designed by architect Henry Bacon, who is best known for the Lincoln Memorial. (Courtesy of the Paterson Museum, Paterson, New Jersey.)

The library building remains one of the most important architectural statements of Paterson's grand era and served as a focus of community engagement, including a World War I book drive, shown above. The library system was more comprehensive than simply the Broadway main library. Branches were established in the neighborhoods to serve local areas. By 1917, there were branches on Grand Street and in the Totowa, Riverside, and People's Park neighborhoods. While the main branch was the largest facility, the other branches were important in fostering the neighborhoods. None had the architectural presence of the main branch. (Both, courtesy of the Paterson Museum, Paterson, New Jersey.)

Health care services in Paterson were originated by ethnic and religious communities. The initial health care system was started by the Roman Catholic Sisters of Mercy, who founded St. Joseph's Hospital in 1867. The original clinic was in the downtown area on Church Street between Market and Ellison Streets. St. Joseph's quickly outgrew the site and relocated to an area on Main Street near the Newark railroad crossing, where it remains. The hospital served all the citizens of the city, including the indigent population, and has continuously expanded its facilities. Over the years, St. Joseph's has remained the city's anchor health care institution. (Both, courtesy of the Paterson Museum, Paterson, New Jersey.)

In the 1870s, women from the city's prominent churches began meetings to consider founding a second hospital in the city. They were especially concerned with providing health care for women. The group formed the Ladies Hospital Association, and that organization grew into Paterson General Hospital. The organization purchased the Lynch Farm in 1872 and began a construction program supported by Paterson's most successful merchants and business owners. The Paterson General Hospital was an important factor in the city's health care system for generations. (Courtesy of the Paterson Museum, Paterson, New Jersey.)

Paterson General Hospital grew to become a comprehensive primary health care provider with an emphasis on women's health issues, including "lying in." The Quackenbush School of Nursing was part of the Paterson General Hospital campus. The eye and ear clinic was another specialized service found at the general hospital. The Paterson General Hospital moved to Wayne, New Jersey, in the 1970s and is now part of the St. Joseph's Hospital System. (Both, courtesy of the Paterson Museum, Paterson, New Jersey.)

Completing the picture of the major health care institutions in Paterson is the Barnert Memorial Hospital, an institution that grew out of a small clinic on Broadway. Nathan Barnert, a successful businessman and leader of the Jewish community, wanted to honor his wife, Miriam, who died in 1902. A clinic was started in the former home of Henry Crosby (shown previously) on Broadway and expanded into a full-service hospital that commenced construction in 1914 and opened in 1916. Consequently, each of the major religious groups in the city of Paterson had a hospital that was suited to their requirements. (Courtesy of the Paterson Museum, Paterson, New Jersey.)

The Paterson Armory stood on Market Street directly across the street from Paterson General Hospital. The armory was built under a law passed in 1889, and the cornerstone was placed on Memorial Day 1894. The site was the home of New Jersey's 2nd Regiment and was opened in 1896. The fortress-like building contained 53,800 square feet. The crenellated three-story brick and steel structure was used for military mobilizations, political and labor rallies, sporting events, circuses, and a range of other activities for years. It was damaged in a fire in 2015 and subsequently demolished. (Both, courtesy of the Paterson Museum, Paterson, New Jersey.)

In 1892, the YMCA of Paterson occupied the former Cooke home on Ellison Street. Sarah E. Cooke had donated her elegant mansion in memory of her late husband, John Cooke, of the locomotive firm Danforth & Cooke. A building containing baths, bowling alleys, a gymnasium, and an assembly hall was erected behind this facility. The 1902 fire destroyed the YMCA of Paterson. A new facility designed by Fred Wesley Wentworth was erected at 137 Ellison Street, pictured here at left. The new YMCA contained dormitories, a swimming pool, a track, and a library and had a great following. Services included assistance to immigrants and fundraising for American military forces during World War I. Ultimately, the YMCA outgrew this building and replaced it on Ward Street. (Both, courtesy of the Paterson Museum, Paterson, New Jersey.)

The Paterson YMCA relocated to Ward Street in September 1930. The new facility was built at a cost of $1.5 million. During War World II, preinduction physical training was offered to potential military recruits. The facility includes a pool, gymnasium, meeting rooms, and residential rooms that were designed for short-term stays. (Courtesy of the Paterson Museum, Paterson, New Jersey.)

There were parallel social organizations in a variety of areas. Community groups like the Ys were found in a number of neighborhoods. The Paterson YM-YWHA (Young Men's–Young Women's Hebrew Association) was incorporated in 1914 and rented quarters at 97 Broadway. The founders were determined to create a facility to match the existing YMCA, which admitted Jews but only under a quota system. The new YMHA proudly proclaimed, "No quotas here!" In December 1922, the YMHA and the YWHA formed one organization and prepared to move into a new home together in a new Georgian-style building. The institutional classical design was of red brick with granite ornamentation. (Above, courtesy of the Jewish Historical Society of Northern New Jersey; below, courtesy of the Paterson Museum, Paterson, New Jersey.)

Among the most popular and well supported social organizations were Masonic lodges. In the early years, Masonic lodges were spread out throughout the city and were located in commercial buildings and halls. In the late 19th century, specially designed Masonic lodges were developed. The building shown here is a Masonic lodge constructed in the 1890s on Market Street a short distance from the city hall. It was designed by Fred Wesley Wentworth in an English manor style, and its masonry facade protected it from damage during the Great Fire. (Courtesy of the Paterson Museum, Paterson, New Jersey.)

While there have been lodges throughout the city, the growing influence and prosperity of the Masonic movement peaked in the 1920s with a grand new Masonic temple that was erected on Broadway. It housed multiple lodge facilities and served as the center for regional activities. Nathan Barnert was a local leader and Mason as well as a contributor to the new construction. The photograph above shows him in a top hat and tails at the cornerstone ceremony for the new Broadway building in October 1922. The photograph below shows the completed facility. (Both, courtesy of the Paterson Museum, Paterson, New Jersey.)

During the period between 1860 and 1920, the ways in which goods and people moved through the city evolved from horse and carriage to fully mechanized cars, trucks, and buses. The changes reflect the most transformational period in modern history. The colorful images of the period tell a great story of how the system evolved in Paterson. The horse-drawn vehicles of the Paterson Washing Company lined up in front of the plant offers a striking representation of the early years of urban transportation. The Pillsbury Flour truck, on its way to a commercial bakery in Paterson, offers meaning to the term "two horsepower." The beasts of burden had more than their share of hard work to feed the locals. (Both, courtesy of the Paterson Museum, Paterson, New Jersey.)

The arrival of mechanized transportation in the early 1900s is shown with the emergence of basic trucks and vans that replaced the horse-drawn carriages. Here is the beer truck of the Feigenspan brand—the "beer that builds." The Great Eastern Stores, a local group of groceries, proudly show off their newest vehicles below, the precursor of today's step vans and delivery trucks. (Both, courtesy of the Paterson Museum, Paterson, New Jersey.

Local businesses brought their goods to consumers in their newly designed and colorful trucks. Kleen Maid was at the forefront of this new type of retailing, and its vans were rolling advertisements for its wares. These luxury buses made their way from Paterson to Gimbel's Department Store in Herald Square. This service was offered on local roads that were primitive by today's standards. In the years before modern highways, bus services were secondary to local train service, and Paterson was connected to the region by the Erie Lackawanna and the Susquehanna Railroads. (Both, courtesy of the Paterson Museum, Paterson, New Jersey.)

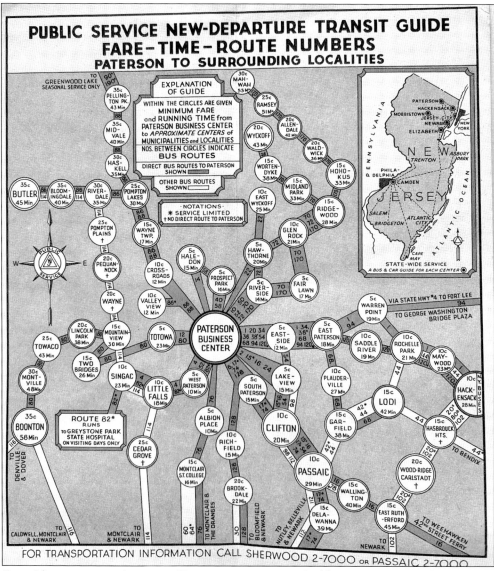

One of the competitive advantages of Paterson was its system of public transportation and connections to other locations in the region. Paterson drew on its surrounding urban and suburban communities for customers for its stores, theaters, banks, and institutions. With the decline in large-scale industrial production, the city became home to hundreds of smaller businesses that were able to draw their workforce via trains and buses. This network was essential until the late 1960s and 1970s, when this network was systematically dismantled by the construction of Interstate 80, which cut a swath through the city and then isolated it. Add the growth of highway-oriented retail and the new malls, and the consequences ripple through the city to this date. (Courtesy of the Rutgers University Historical Maps of New Jersey.)

BIBLIOGRAPHY

Adler, William M. *Mollie's Job: The Story of Life and Work on the Global Assembly Line*. New York: Scribner, 2001.

Corbett, Glenn P. *The Great Paterson Fire of 1902: The Story of New Jersey's Biggest Blaze*. Privately published, Pompton Plains, NJ, 2002.

Golin, Steve. *The Fragile Bridge: Paterson Silk Strike 1913*. Philadelphia, PA: Temple University Press, 1988.

Gutman, Herbert G. "The Reality of Rags-to-Riches 'Myth': The Case of Paterson, New Jersey, Locomotive, Iron, and Machinery Manufacturers, 1830–1880." In *Nineteenth-Century Cities: Essays in the New Urban History*, edited by Stephan Thernstrom and Richard Sennett, 98–124. New Haven, CT: Yale University, 1969.

Herbst, John A., and Catherine Keene. *Life and Times in Silk City: A Photographic Essay of Paterson, New Jersey*. Haledon, NJ: The American Labor Museum, 1984.

Johnson, Paul E. *Sam Patch, the Famous Jumper*. New York: Hill and Wang, 2003.

Nelson, William, and Charles A. Shriner. *History of Paterson and Its Environs (The Silk City)*. Three volumes. New York: Lewis Historical Publishing Company, 1920.

Norwood, Christopher. *About Paterson*. New York: E.P. Dutton, 1974.

Polton, Richard E. *The Life and Times of Fred Wesley Wentworth: The Architect Who Shaped Paterson, NJ and Its People*. Montclair, NJ: Pine Hill Press, 2012.

Read, Philip M. *Paterson*. Charleston, SC: Arcadia Publishing, 2003.

Schwartz, Cipora O. *An American Jewish Odyssey: American Religious Freedom and the Nathan Barnert Memorial Temple*. Jersey City, NJ: Ktav Publishing House, 2007.

Shriner, Charles, A. *Paterson, New Jersey, Illustrated: Its Advantages for Manufacturing and Residence: Its Industries, Prominent Men, Banks, School, Churches, Etc*. Paterson, NJ: The Press Printing and Publishing Company, 1890.

Trumbull, I.R. *A History of Industrial Paterson: Being a Compendium of the Establishment, Growth and Present Status in Paterson, NJ*. Privately published, Paterson, NJ, 1882.

Wallace, Edith B. *"An Incorporation of the Adventurers": A History of the Society of Establishing Useful Manufactures, Paterson "Silk City" and Its People, and the Great Falls of the Passaic River: Historic Resource Study*. National Park Service, US Department of the Interior, December 2019.

Wallerstein, Jane. *Voices from the Paterson Silk Mills*. Charleston, SC: Arcadia Publishing, 2002.

DISCOVER THOUSANDS OF LOCAL HISTORY BOOKS FEATURING MILLIONS OF VINTAGE IMAGES

Arcadia Publishing, the leading local history publisher in the United States, is committed to making history accessible and meaningful through publishing books that celebrate and preserve the heritage of America's people and places.

Find more books like this at
www.arcadiapublishing.com

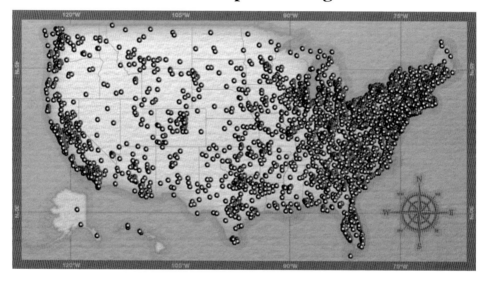

Search for your hometown history, your old stomping grounds, and even your favorite sports team.

Consistent with our mission to preserve history on a local level, this book was printed in South Carolina on American-made paper and manufactured entirely in the United States. Products carrying the accredited Forest Stewardship Council (FSC) label are printed on 100 percent FSC-certified paper.

MADE IN THE
USA